Information Sy

SSADM and Capacity Planning

Alun David

CCTA

April 1992

LONDON: HMSO

© Crown Copyright 1992

Applications for reproduction should be made to HMSO

First published 1992

ISBN 0 11 330577 X

For further information regarding this publication and other CCTA products please contact:

Library
Riverwalk House
157-161 Millbank
London SW7P 4RT

071-217 3331

Contents

Foreword

1 Introduction   1
    1.1 Purpose of this volume
    1.2 Who should read this volume
    1.3 Structure of this volume

2 Overview   3
    2.1 Background
    2.2 Structured Systems Analysis and Design Method (SSADM)
    2.3 Capacity planning
    2.4 Capacity planning and SSADM

3 Using capacity planning in an SSADM environment   11
    3.1 Why should capacity planning be used during analysis and design?
    3.2 Interfaces with SSADM
    3.3 Preparation for capacity planning
    3.4 The capacity planning process
    3.5 The results, their evaluation and feedback to SSADM
    3.6 What to do if capacity planning expertise is not available

4 The interface between SSADM and capacity planning   21
    4.1 Technical System Options (Stage 4)
    4.2 Logical Design (Stage 5)
    4.3 Physical Design (Stage 6)

Annexes **31**

    A   SSADM Stage 4 (Technical System Options) information sources

    B   SSADM Stage 5 (Logical Design) information sources

    C   SSADM Stage 6 (Physical Design) information sources

Bibliography **39**

Glossary **41**

Foreword

The **Information Systems Engineering Library** provides guidance on carrying out Information Systems Engineering activities. In the IS lifecycle, Information Systems Engineering takes place once the IS strategy has been defined. It is concerned with the development of information systems up to the operational stage, when an information system becomes the responsibility of infrastructure management.

The Information Systems Engineering Library builds on the guidance in the CCTA IS Guides B set: *Developing Information Systems* and complements other CCTA products, in particular the IS project management method, PRINCE, and the systems analysis and design method, SSADM.

The Information Systems Engineering Library will be of interest to IS providers, helping them to improve the quality and productivity of their IS development work. It will also be of interest to business managers, whose business operations depend on having effective IS support by means of Information Systems Engineering activities.

CCTA welcomes customer views on Information Systems Engineering Library publications. Please send your comments to:

Customer Services
Information Systems Engineering Group
Gildengate House
Upper Green Lane
Norwich NR3 1DW.

Acknowledgements

The assistance of Cathy Morton under contract to CCTA from Model Systems Ltd is gratefully acknowledged.

The assistance of CCTA staff Brian Johnson and Roy Longbottom is also gratefully acknowledged.

1 Introduction

1.1 Purpose of this volume

This volume is intended to explain how capacity planning techniques are used in SSADM projects for the development of new information systems.

Capacity planning is used to determine the optimum balance between *capacity* – which costs money – and performance-related *service quality*. This helps the organisation to make an informed decision about the right quality and cost balance to meet its business needs.

Capacity planning can also be used to help SSADM practitioners to optimise the design of an information system in terms of performance.

1.2 Who should read this volume

This volume is primarily intended for people involved in SSADM projects who wish to make use of capacity planning techniques. It should be of particular interest to SSADM practitioners and capacity planners.

The volume should also be of interest to tool suppliers for SSADM and capacity planning, providing them with opportunities to develop new tools.

1.3 Structure of this volume

Chapter 2 provides an overview of the volume. Chapter 3 describes how capacity planning techniques are used in an SSADM environment, with advice on what can be achieved if there is no capacity planning expertise available. Chapter 4 details the SSADM Stages and Steps and information products relevant to capacity planning. The Annexes contain the detailed mapping between the SSADM information sources and the information needs of capacity planning.

SSADM and Capacity Planning

2 Overview

2.1 Background

Capacity planning techniques have been used for some time to assess the effects of workload changes on the performance of existing information systems and to identify the hardware capacity needed to support required service levels – transaction throughput and response time.

Information systems are often designed with little emphasis on Service Level Requirements (SLRs) and with only cursory regard for their potential size and the impact they might have on existing information systems running alongside them on the same IT infrastructure. Capacity planning techniques used during the analysis and design of a new system allow SLRs to be taken fully into account. Information is provided on the hardware capacity needed to meet required service levels, both for the new systems and for any existing systems running alongside on the same hardware. To look at the information another way, the service levels that can be supported on a given hardware platform can be predicted. The effects on service levels of changes to the hardware configuration or the functionality of the system can be predicted, thus allowing the organisation to get the right balance between business needs (service quality) and the cost of providing the service.

The linking of capacity planning and SSADM provides opportunities for SSADM practitioners to predict either the levels of service that the new information system can provide (on a given hardware configuration) or the hardware configuration needed to support the required service levels.

IT service providers will have earlier and more precise information about new workloads to be accommodated. Therefore earlier and more precise information is available about the service levels to be achieved and/or the hardware capacity needed to achieve them.

2.2 Structured Systems Analysis and Design Method (SSADM)

SSADM is the UK government's preferred method for the systems analysis and design of IT based information systems. The method covers the part of the information system life cycle from Feasibility Study to Physical Design.

SSADM is a six stage method, illustrated in Figure 1 opposite. The Feasibility Study, Stage 0, uses an abbreviated version of Stages 1 – 3 to define the user requirement. The full SSADM Study uses Stages 1 – 6. Although the opening SSADM Stages covering Requirements Definition are driven by the users or *demand side*, as a method SSADM is in the province of the IS providers, or *supply side*.

SSADM concentrates on the functional definition of an information system; it does not have techniques for assessing the performance of the system in terms of throughput and response times.

2.3 Capacity planning

Capacity planning is part of Capacity Management, a discipline in the IT Services area. For further information and guidance on capacity management, see the IT Infrastructure Library module *Capacity Management*.

Capacity planning techniques are used to help organisations predict hardware capacity requirements and decide the right performance/cost balance for their needs. They are also used to influence the design of systems to optimise their performance and that of other systems sharing the same hardware.

Capacity planning thus helps organisations to:

- provide information system services of the required quality at the best price
- reduce the risk that new systems going 'live' will perform unsatisfactorily or that existing systems will start to perform badly
- contain the costs of providing information systems.

Chapter 2
Overview

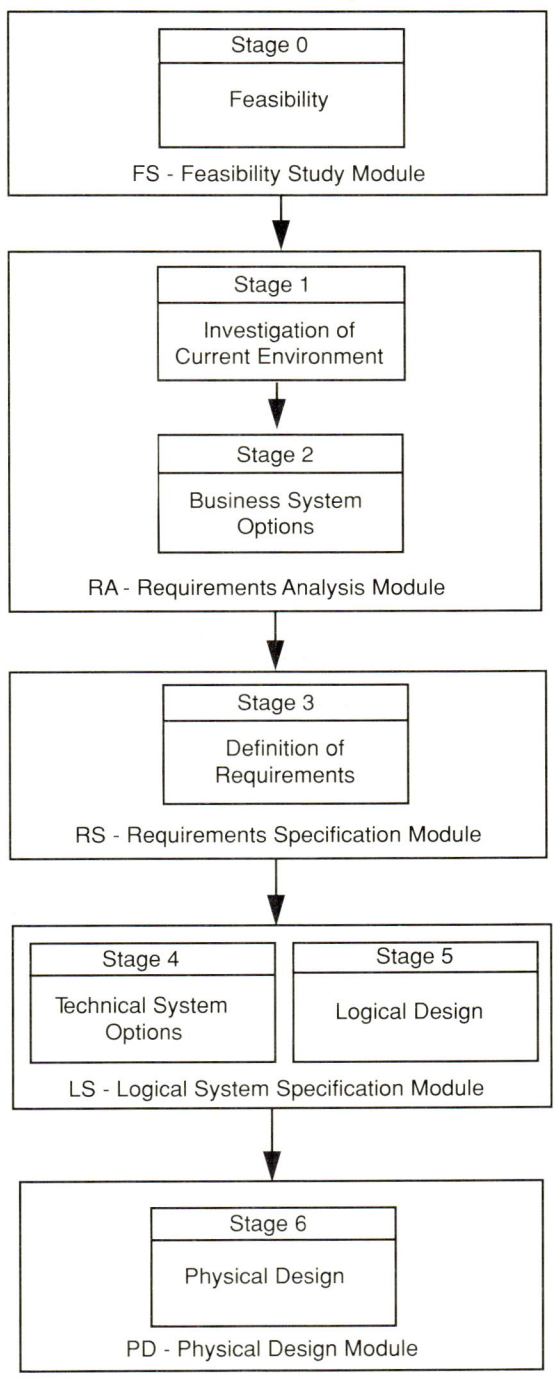

Figure 1: Modules and Stages of SSADM

Because capacity planning can be used to predict the capacity requirements and performance of systems while they are being developed, it helps organisations to validate their cost/benefit assumptions for new information systems early in the lifecycle, when errors and problems can be corrected more cheaply.

The capacity planning team must liaise with the SSADM project team to obtain the information needed to predict the hardware resources that will be required to run the new application. This predicts whether it meets its Service Level Requirements or whether these have to be modified so that the system can be implemented on the existing hardware configuration, while ensuring that the service levels of any existing systems that are to share the hardware can be maintained. The information obtained from the SSADM project can be used by the capacity planning team to produce a recommendation on how to optimise the proposed design so that it needs the minimum amount of hardware resources or delivers the best performance.

Effective capacity planning requires the use of specialist software tools for computers and networks. It is difficult to achieve good results using manual methods. The choice of tool is controlled very much by what is available in the installation and SSADM practitioners may have to mould their demands and the information they supply for capacity planning purposes to what different tools can provide. The advice in this guide can, however, easily be applied to the requirements imposed by any of the available tools. Because, at present, these tools are aimed at specialist capacity planners, capacity planning expertise is usually required to interpret the results to make them meaningful to users and SSADM practitioners.

Capacity planning tools investigate the relationship between workloads, the hardware configurations on which they run and delivered service levels, using modelling techniques. (See the IT Infrastructure Library module *Capacity Management* for more information.) Some suppliers of capacity planning tools offer 'front-ends' which facilitate the modelling of information systems during their design and development. Many tools run on a PC but some require mainframe support.

Chapter 2
Overview

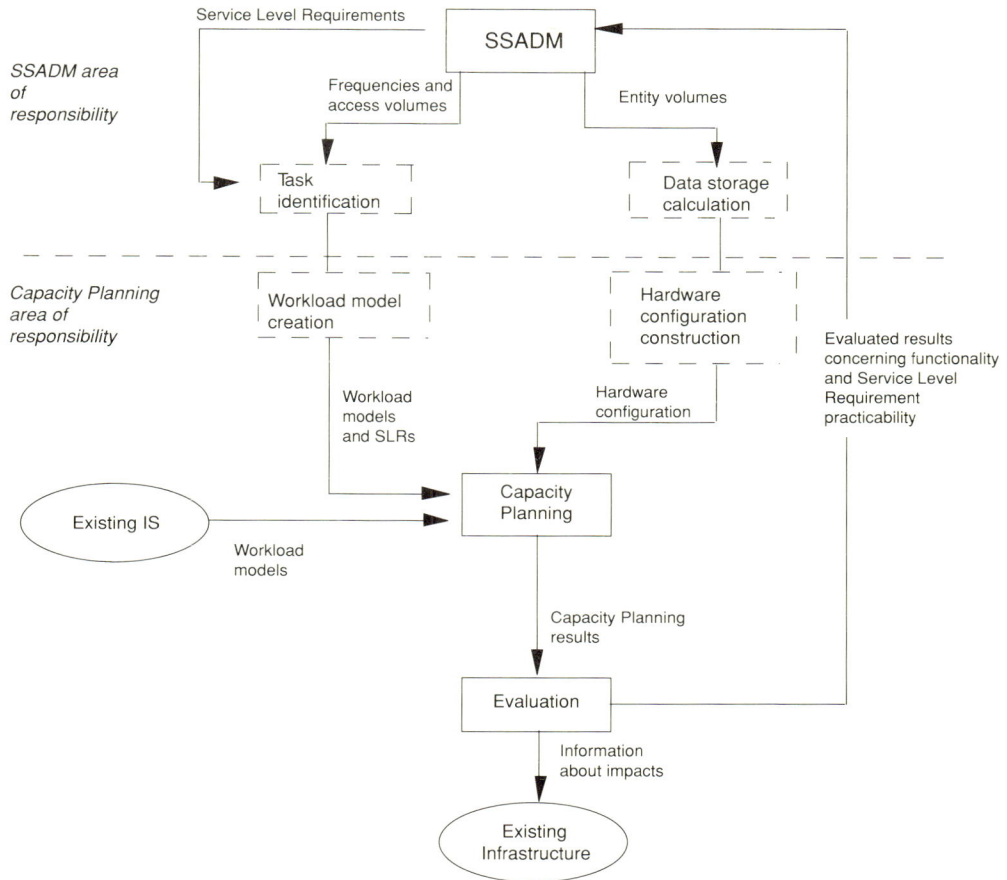

Figure 2: Areas of responsibility and included activities

2.4	**Capacity planning and SSADM**	The use of capacity planning techniques during an SSADM project imposes new responsibilities on both the SSADM practitioners and capacity planners. Figure 2 shows both the existing and the new activities, indicating the general area within which they are placed. These new activities are allocated as the responsibility of either the SSADM or the capacity planning practitioner. Both sets of practitioners need to contribute.

The SSADM practitioner is responsible for the activities shown in Figure 2 within the SSADM area of responsibility. This involves identifying the tasks in the new system to be converted into workloads for the capacity planning exercise and ensuring that all the information required from SSADM is available for capacity planning.

The capacity planner takes responsibility for building the models of the workloads from the tasks and of the hardware configurations, as described in the IT Infrastructure Library module *Capacity Management*. The information supplied from SSADM sources needs to be augmented by the capacity planner, using experience and knowledge of the installation.

When a modelling exercise is complete the capacity planner has as output a set of service level predictions for the proposed workload running on the proposed hardware configuration. If the predictions are insufficient to meet the SLRs, there are three options:

- change the hardware configuration
- change the workload
- change the SLRs.

In practice, if the workloads and SLRs cannot be accommodated on hardware that the organisation is prepared to afford, then the organisation will have to accept reduced workload or reduced SLRs. The options available to the organisation can be explored iteratively, by feeding different hardware configurations and workloads into the capacity planning tool and observing the effect on predicted SLRs.

The hardware configurations should generally be designed with an upgrade capability, to ensure that any future workload growth can be accommodated.

The SSADM development team takes the information from each capacity planning exercise in turn during Stage 4 and analyses it to determine whether changes to the system specification are feasible or desirable. The SSADM team puts the results of each capacity planning exercise and of any subsequent analysis by the SSADM team to the users in the form of a series of Technical System Options and helps the users to select the most suitable option.

Capacity planning can be used in Stage 6 to help perform some of the SSADM tasks and can also be used for review purposes.

Chapter 2
Overview

The capacity planners must take account of the existing IT infrastructure and of the existing systems that are to run alongside the proposed new system. Hardware upgrades may be needed to ensure that existing Service Level Agreements are maintained (see the IT Infrastructure Library module *Capacity Management* for further details).

3 Using capacity planning techniques in an SSADM environment

3.1 Why should capacity planning be used during analysis and design?

Up until now information systems have been specified largely on the basis of the functionality to be provided. There has been less emphasis placed on the required levels of service that the application should deliver in order to satisfy the needs of the business. As organisations become more dependent on IS, the quality of delivery services assumes growing importance. Adherence to SLRs is a fundamental criterion of service quality. It is therefore essential that information systems should in future be designed to meet the organisation's required service levels.

For detailed guidance on the provision of IS services in accordance with SLRs, please refer to the IT Infrastructure Library module *Service Level Management*.

For the purposes of this volume the important service levels are those related to the required performance of the system: task arrival rates, response times and throughput. In capacity planning terms, arrival rates are a characteristic of a workload and are *inputs* to capacity planning exercises, whereas the other SLRs are *outputs* (see Figure 3).

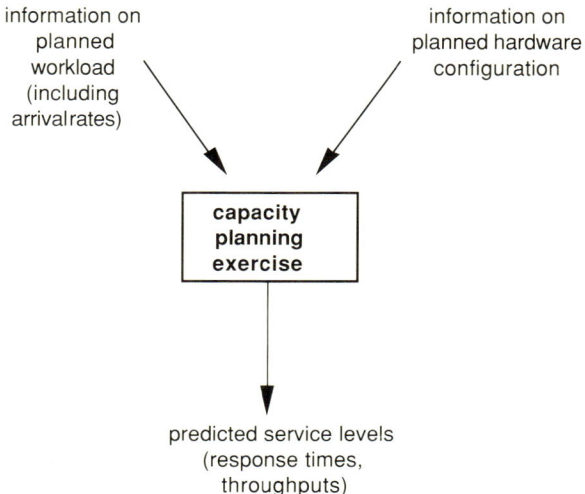

Figure 3: Inputs and outputs of a capacity planning exercise

If predicted service levels do not meet required service levels when a capacity planning exercise is carried out, the exercise is rerun with different hardware configurations and/or workloads, or the required service levels are revised until a solution acceptable to users and service providers is reached.

Other Service Level Requirements such as availability are equally important but cannot be fully addressed by means of a capacity planning approach. (See the IT Infrastructure Library module *Availability Management* for more information.)

During systems analysis and design, the required service levels are referred to as *service level objectives*. As these objectives become more firmly established during the analysis and design phase they are formalised as *Service Level Requirements*. These in turn, as part of the process of implementation and acceptance, are incorporated in a *Service Level Agreement*.

Capacity planning is used to help the SSADM team to design systems that provide a basis for services of the right quality and at the right cost, with the minimum risk of capacity or performance-related problems. Specifically, capacity planning offers the following benefits during analysis and design by:

- providing information on how much hardware is needed to support SLRs (and how much it is going to cost). This allows the team to decide if the projected hardware solution is viable or whether they should seek lesser SLRs (that is, are the SLRs practical and reasonable?)
- helping the team to optimise the design to obtain the best service for the minimum hardware
- reducing the risk that the new system will not work because of inadequate hardware
- helping to ensure that hardware upgrades are controlled
- helping to ensure that existing SLAs for systems running alongside the new ones are not jeopardised.

Chapter 3
Using capacity planning techniques in an SSADM environment

Although the results of capacity planning are only *estimates*, the benefits to be gained from the recommended approach reduce risk and uncertainty. The use of capacity planning techniques as described here should result in markedly better predictions of the capacity needed to support required service levels. The accuracy of the predictions depends on the accuracy of the data input to the capacity planning tools.

3.2   Interfaces with SSADM At specific points in the SSADM process capacity planning techniques can be used to assess the service levels that are achievable for the new system. Figure 4 shows the points at which information is passed between the users, the SSADM development team and capacity planners.

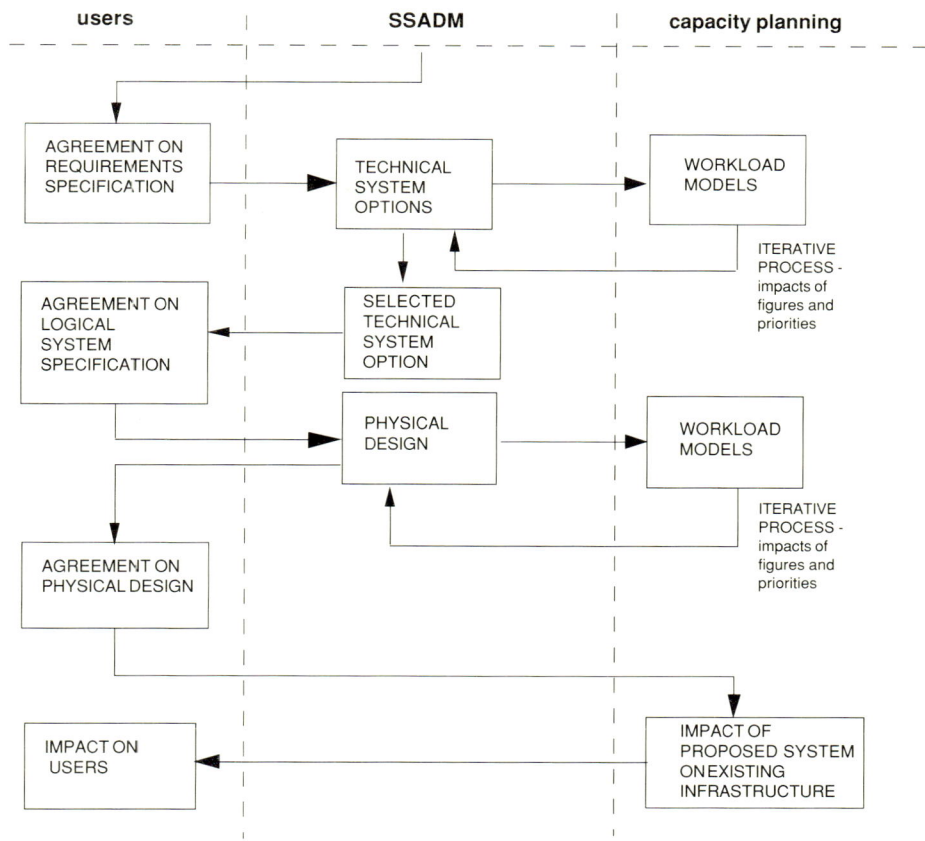

Figure 4: Evaluation of the capacity planning process

13

To be effective, these interface points must satisfy the following conditions:

- information being available to build workload models and assess hardware configurations
- Service Level Requirements described for each workload
- Technical Environment Descriptions or similar information being available.

The interface points between SSADM and capacity planning are described fully in Chapter 4.

3.3 Preparation for capacity planning

During analysis and design, the following activities are carried out to prepare for and provide outputs to the capacity planning process:

- calculation of data storage requirement
- identification of workloads to be modelled
- descriptions of workloads, with details of on-line task arrival rate or batch concurrency level, number of accesses made to each device, amount of processor usage per task, response and turnaround times.

The data storage requirements are established during the SSADM process by reference to the Logical Data Model. Similarly, the processing workloads can be identified from the SSADM Function Definitions.

3.3.1 Data storage estimation

To estimate the disk data storage requirements of a new system from the information held in the Logical Data Model, the total requirement of each entity (its length multiplied by the number of occurrences) is calculated and all the totals are added together, making allowances for indexing, security and other overheads.

The topic is covered in greater depth in the IT Infrastructure Library module *Capacity Management*.

3.3.2 Identification of workloads

This activity requires judgement and experience to make best use of the information available about a system at different stages in its design and development. The SSADM practitioner establishes from the Function Definitions which tasks are important enough to be worth modelling.

Chapter 3
Using capacity planning techniques in an SSADM environment

(In this context a *task* is a portion of processing that can range in size from a business transaction to a message-pair. The word is chosen deliberately to avoid the technical precision of *message-pair* and the ambiguity of *transaction*. Please refer to the IT Infrastructure Library module *Capacity Management* for further information.)

The purpose of modelling a task is to determine the resources and/or service levels that it will require. All the tasks with given performance characteristics are grouped together as a workload for input to a capacity planning exercise.

On the basis that 80% of the capacity will be consumed by 20% of the tasks, these tasks form the basis of the modelling. The systems analysts, users, and capacity planners must decide, using the Requirements Catalogue, on the relative importance of different tasks to decide which ones comprise that 20%.

A general guideline is that all long-running and all frequently used tasks must be included. It is important to include all complex transactions, even if they are infrequently invoked. The capacity planning exercise will not be worth much if, for example, an end of period report takes several days to run, during which time other users are denied access.

3.3.3 Workload description

For each workload to be modelled the required inputs are likely to be:

- the rate at which on-line tasks arrive to be processed or the concurrency level of batch jobs

- the number of accesses made to each type of device

- the total amount of processor usage, expressed in seconds

- the required response or turnaround time.

On-line task arrival rate or batch concurrency level

This information is derived from the frequency information held in SSADM documentation. The Annexes to this volume provide detailed information on where the appropriate SSADM products can be found. The probability of each task occurring must also be estimated. The frequencies stated may need to be interpreted to provide information about peaks or troughs in frequency.

Number of accesses made to each device	One necessary assumption is that the only devices accessed are disk units – it is difficult to predict other accesses with any degree of accuracy from SSADM sources. The number of accesses made to each device is equivalent to the number of logical disk accesses. Because the entity is the basis of data definition in SSADM, the number of entity accesses has to be converted to the number of logical disk accesses.

To make this conversion, the important considerations are access priorities, size of database area or file sizes, and installation standards.

The number of entity accesses or *effects per task* needs to be established. The process of establishing the number of effects per task involves:

- deciding on the entities affected
- assessing the probability of each effect taking place
- multiplying the probability by the number of effects
- producing the sum of all the individual totals to give the number of effects on entities.

Last, the number of effects requires conversion to the number of physical disk accesses.

The type of logical access can affect the number of physical accesses actually made. For example, a serial read will cause fewer physical accesses than a chained database insertion. The conversion is carried out as a 'rule of thumb' exercise based either on experience or on investigation of the proposed system software and hardware. Some software packages incorporate algorithms to perform this conversion. |
| Amount of processor usage per task | IT based information systems for business are generally input/output bound rather than processor bound. In general, it is reasonable to assume that the computational processor activity is minimal and can be disregarded, though this may not always be the case. Each database access will involve processor activity; different types of access (Read, Insert, Modify or Delete) may involve different levels of activity. |

Chapter 3
Using capacity planning techniques in an SSADM environment

The numbers of each type of access per task require to be counted and will need to be converted by the capacity planner to a value for processor occupancy in seconds. This information is hardware-specific. One approach to making this conversion is to:

- find out the number of machine instructions needed for each physical disk access
- multiply it by the number of disk accesses
- divide by the processor 'MIP' rating, giving an approximate value for the number of seconds of processor occupancy per task.

As with conversion from entity effects to physical disk accesses, some capacity planning software packages contain algorithms supporting this transformation.

Response and turnaround times

Each transaction processing task and batch job under development requires the levels of service to be considered and gradually consolidated. The user wants to know how quickly the task is expected to provide a response or may specify how long it is expected to take. The IT manager wants to know what response and turnaround times can be achieved for the predicted transaction arrival rates and batch jobs concurrency levels. Throughput rates can be calculated from this information. Required service levels are obtained from the SSADM Function Definitions and Requirements Catalogue; achievable service levels then have to be calculated with capacity planning techniques.

3.4 The capacity planning process

The workload information obtained as in section 3.3 is fed into the capacity planning process along with information about the proposed hardware configuration. The process is carried out iteratively until satisfactory service levels are achievable on affordable hardware.

No two capacity modelling tools use exactly the same information. Chapter 4 and the Annexes describe where relevant information may be found and when it is used.

The results of capacity modelling are compared with the Service Level Requirements (SLRs) and the results of this comparison fed back into the SSADM process. A number of iterations may be required until the predicted levels of service match the SLRs. (This matching may involve changing the SLRs.) These SLRs are included in the Requirements Catalogue and Function Definitions. They should provide all the information needed for the evaluation of capacity planning results. If not, the SLRs are used as a basis for the development of fuller detail.

3.5 The results, their evaluation and feedback to SSADM

Capacity planning output describes throughput, response times and the anticipated rate of hardware component usage for each workload.

The capacity planner interprets the results of modelling and produces a comparison of the required service levels with those predicted by the model in a way that is meaningful to the SSADM practitioner.

This gives information to both the development team and users, showing how closely the original design objectives are being met. The following questions have to be answered:

- are the objectives achievable?
- are the objectives reasonable?

It may be necessary to review the SLRs with the users and change them if necessary so that satisfactory objectives can be achieved at optimum cost.

The capacity planners can use the information about hardware component usage to optimise the design of the hardware configuration by identifying the system components likely to prove critical. Two techniques used in the SSADM process are available to help:

- *Sensitivity Analysis*, the ability to process 'what if' speculative models, permits experimentation with different solutions to the hardware configuration needed to support an information system and gives an opportunity to select the most appropriate

- *Impact Analysis*, modelling the proposed information system, provides a more accurate and complete picture of anticipated size and possible effects on both the user area and the existing IT infrastructure.

	SSADM Stage 4	The development team should now have sufficient information to balance the desired objectives against the expected costs. They produce a description of how well the system will meet the design objectives and required service levels. This description indicates the estimated range of costs to the users.
		The description is also useful to the IT service providers. They need to know that new applications can be accommodated on the existing infrastructure (if necessary) without straining existing services or violating their Service Level Agreements.
	SSADM Stage 6	Capacity planning is also used in SSADM Stage 6 as a review mechanism, and is used to help to perform some of the SSADM tasks.
3.6	**What to do if capacity planning expertise is not available**	If the SSADM team is working in an environment where capacity planning expertise is not available, the problem of how best to obtain and retain it needs to be considered. However, there may be situations in which such expertise cannot be obtained within a reasonable timescale. This topic is discussed in the IT Infrastructure Library module *Capacity Management* in the annex on capacity and performance problems in greenfield sites. It provides 'rules of thumb' for manual sizing of new applications.
		IT suppliers may be able to provide further information when responding to Operational Requirements – but the project team needs to be very circumspect about using this information.

SSADM and Capacity Planning

4 The interface between SSADM and capacity planning

This chapter describes the information products from the relevant stages of an SSADM project that may be used for capacity planning. In Stage 4 capacity planning is used as a review tool; in Stage 6 it can be used to help to perform some of the SSADM tasks.

These products are used for the calculation of the data storage requirements and the creation of workload models. The chapter also includes diagrammatic descriptions of the interface points between SSADM and capacity planning. The Annexes to this volume contain the information requirements of capacity planning cross-referenced with the relevant SSADM products.

The exchange of information usually begins at SSADM Stage 4, when the Technical Environment Description (TED) is defined. Although it is possible to build workload models using SSADM sources before this point, in practice the information is not generally well enough defined to be useful.

It is recommended that the notes in the following sections are read in conjunction with the diagrams.

4.1 Technical System Options (Stage 4)

4.1.1 Overview of Stage 4

The development of Technical System Options (TSOs) is based on the output from Stage 3, Requirements Specification, which is a development of the Business System Option chosen in Stage 2. TSOs propose different ways of physically implementing the Requirements Specification. Figure 5 (overleaf) shows Stage 4.

The required system is specified. Service Level Requirements and their Cost/Benefit Analyses are now established in readiness for the design phase. There should be sufficient information available to construct a preliminary workload for input to a capacity planning modelling tool. The TED for each Technical System Option allows preliminary hardware configurations to be put together in sufficient detail for input to a capacity planning modelling tool.

SSADM and Capacity Planning

Module LS : Logical System Specification
Stage 4 : Technical System Options

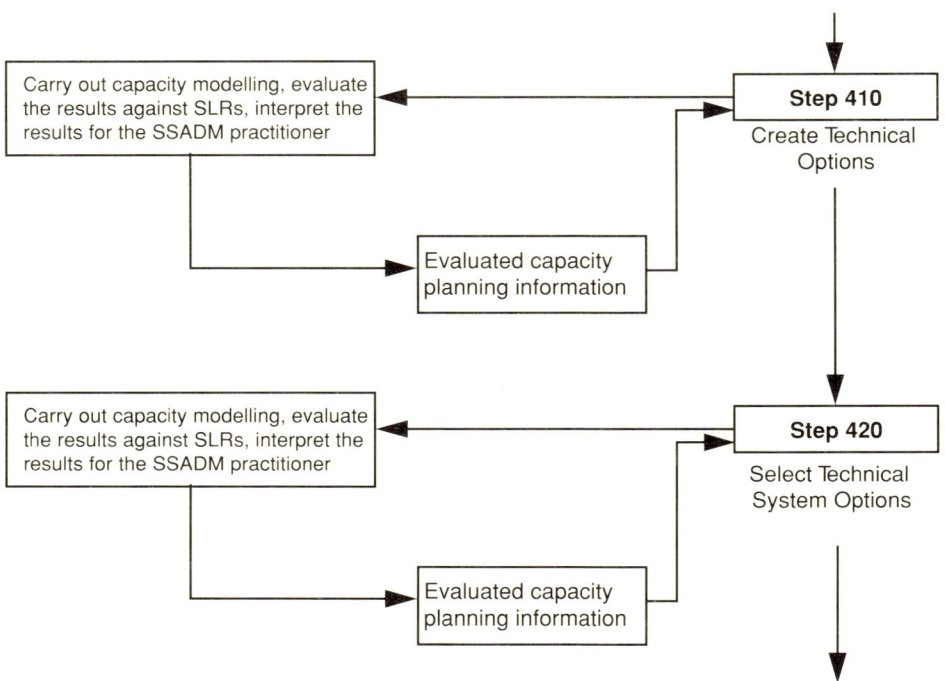

Figure 5: SSADM Stage 4 Technical System Options

4.1.2 When to use capacity planning

Capacity planning techniques are used in the selection of a Technical System Option to:

- help assess the likely technical environments that can support the Requirements Specification without degrading Service Level Requirements (SLRs)
- assess the practicability of desired SLRs
- provide assistance with Cost/Benefit and Impact Analyses.

Capacity planning can be of value at two points during this stage, depending on the scale of the proposed information system – Step 410 and Step 420.

Step 410

At this point capacity planning is used to assist in the selection of a Technical System Option. If the project is large enough, it may prove worthwhile to carry out capacity modelling on each candidate TSO. The capacity planning results for each TSO are evaluated against the Service Level Requirements. This serves both to verify the feasibility of the service levels and to provide a basis on which to judge each option. The capacity planning output contributes to the development of the Cost/Benefit and Impact Analyses for each option.

Step 420

Once a TSO has been selected capacity modelling confirms whether the selected option supports the specified service levels. If the service levels are not met by the selected option the SSADM practitioner can recommend one of four options:

- adjust service levels
- adjust the TSO
- reduce the functionality to be provided
- adjust the cost constraints.

Information produced by capacity planning is input to the Cost/Benefit and Impact Analyses for the chosen option.

4.1.3 Calculation of data storage requirements

Each TSO includes an outline Technical Environment Description (TED), which describes a proposed hardware configuration on which the system could be implemented. Although the TED is an SSADM product, it is more dependent on information sources outside the method for its development than on information gathered and processed using SSADM itself. One part of the TED requiring input from SSADM is the data storage requirement which is calculated using the volumetric information in the Entity Descriptions and the Data Catalogue. However this data storage requirement should reflect the size of the entities and consideration should be given to which entities need to be stored together because they are frequently accessed together. This information is input to capacity planning (see section 3.3.1).

4.1.4 Creation of workload models

By the time Stage 3 is complete, all of the volumetric data about the required system should be held in the Requirements Specification; check that this is the case and try to remedy any omissions.

The task arrival rates are estimated using information from the Function Definitions. The number of disk accesses for each task are then calculated from the numbers of entity effects. These are not documented explicitly in SSADM but can be derived from several SSADM sources and should be noted on the Effect Correspondence Diagrams (ECDs). Similarly, the amount of processing required for the task is estimated using the number of entity effects on the ECDs.

The ECD gives the structure of an event, including the correspondence between effects, iterated effects and optional effects. By looking at the entity volumes, documented in the Entity Descriptions, together with the ECD structure and the input data on the I/O Structure most of the numbers of effect occurrences can be derived. For example if a master and all its details are deleted by an event the number of effect occurrences for the detail will be the same as the number of details per master.

The input data and the comments recorded on the I/O Structures can also help in determining effect occurrences. The I/O Structure diagrams show optional and iterated input data. The comments on the I/O Structure Description record the circumstances under which data is optional and the expected number of iterations.

There are occasions where the number of effect occurrences cannot be derived from these sources. This is where an effect is dependent on a condition which can

Chapter 4
The interface between SSADM and capacity planning

only be tested by looking at the database. In these cases the SSADM practitioner must determine the probability of the effect occurring through discussion with the user. It is recommended that the SSADM practitioner notes all the effect volumetrics on the ECD to be passed to the capacity planner.

Although Dialogue Structures are not created until Stage 5 the dialogues to be built are identified in the User/Role Function Matrix produced in Stage 3. The critical functions must be decided upon. The complexity of the dialogues may be determined from the working documentation for prototyping, if it has been produced. I/O Structures can also be used to gain an impression of the complexity of the dialogues.

4.1.5 Information sources

Annex A lists the capacity planning information requirements cross-referenced with the relevant SSADM products and the entries in those products from which the information can be derived.

4.1.6 Results of the capacity planning exercises

The results of the capacity planning exercises outlined in section 4.1 are evaluated against the performance requirements detailed in the SLRs. This comparison provides a basis for negotiation between the SSADM team, users and service providers. As a result of negotiation adjustments can be made to the required system specification or the SLRs or to the amount of resource available in order to implement the system. If it is considered necessary to re-examine the required system specification or the SLRs further iterations through parts of SSADM may be required.

4.2 Logical Design (Stage 5)

Stage 5 refines the Requirements Specification produced in Stage 3. There should be no new information about requirements; the emphasis is on providing detail for Stage 6. At this point the TED is being developed in Stage 4 as a parallel activity. Capacity planning techniques are not used in this Stage, but may be used at the beginning of Stage 6 if further information becomes available.

SSADM and Capacity Planning

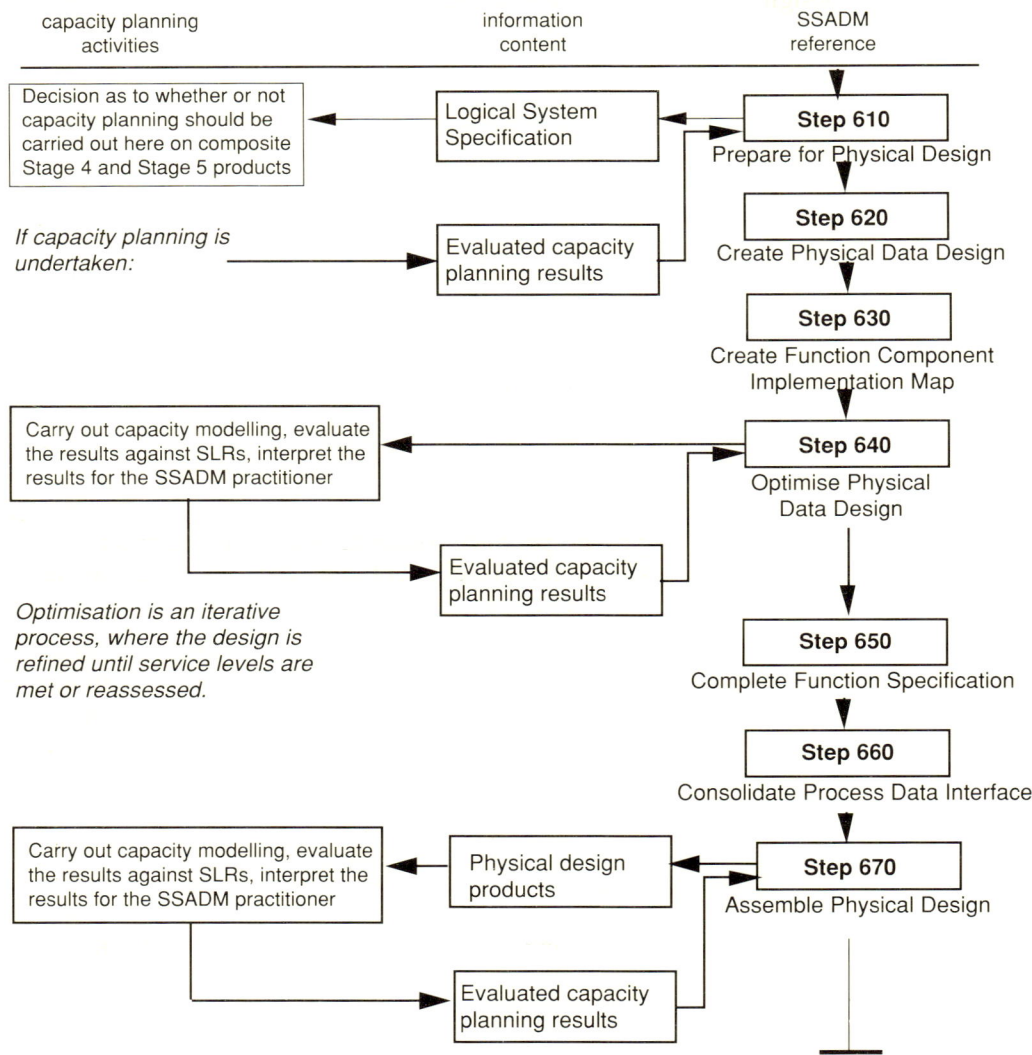

Figure 6: SSADM Stage 6 Physical Design

Chapter 4
The interface between SSADM and capacity planning

4.3 Physical Design (Stage 6)

4.3.1 Overview of Physical Design

In Stage 6 of SSADM the Logical Design is converted into a Physical Design, which specifies how the data and processing are to be implemented in the chosen physical environments. Stage 6 must be customised to suit the physical implementation environment and the project environment. As far as possible the facilities of the target environment, as documented in the Technical Environment Description, should be used to specify the Physical Design. For example, the logical dialogues developed during logical design are transformed into physical specifications using the facilities of the target environment. Figure 6 shows Stage 6.

Because Stage 6 can be configured to meet the requirements of the target environment it is difficult to say exactly when products will be available. However, the latest SSADM products should be the ones that are passed to capacity planning. For example, the SSADM reference manual describes optimisation of the data design being carried out using the logical design process specification products. However, if the physical design process products, documented in the Function Component Implementation Map, are available these should be used.

Similarly, the TED is the SSADM product that describes the target environment, but the SSADM practitioner may have access to the Physical Environment Specification, generally provided by the supplier. This product will be far more detailed than the TED and should be used in preference to the TED. The general rule is to pass to capacity planners the latest and most detailed form of a product.

Although it is difficult to be specific about how and when physical design components will be documented, a general picture can be given of the sort of information that will be available for those components.

4.3.2 When to use capacity planning

The Physical Data Design created in Step 620 is developed in Step 640. It requires the resource times of major functions to be estimated. Capacity planning can be used to investigate whether these estimates can be met using the design. Some target environments support the easy generation of a database and subsequent performance prototyping. If this is so these facilities should be used to assist in optimisation. However, if the target environment does not provide these facilities capacity planning can be used to assist in the development of the Physical Data Design.

There are other Steps within Stage 6 where capacity planning could be used. The designer must balance the cost of carrying out the capacity planning exercise against the perceived benefits and the risks involved in not carrying out the exercise.

Step 610   In this task the designer prepares for physical design. It is not generally recommended that capacity planning is carried out at this point because there is little additional information available to the capacity planners to that supplied in Stage 4. Selection of Technical System Options (Stage 4) and Logical Design (Stage 5) take place in parallel. No new analysis work to develop the specification takes place in Stage 5. However, dialogues will have been developed in Stage 5 and so far have not been input to capacity planning. The designer may decide it is worth carrying out capacity planning at this point so that dialogue information can be included.

Step 640   Capacity planning is used in two tasks within this Step.

Task 640.10   This task estimates the data storage requirements of the system. These can be calculated using capacity planning. The capacity planning results are then evaluated using the storage constraints documented in the Requirements Catalogue. Where storage constraints are not met a decision must be made either to restructure the data design or relax the constraints. This process is repeated until the design meets the storage constraints.

Task 640.20   In this task the resource times of major functions are estimated. Capacity planning can be used to carry out this estimation. The capacity planning results are evaluated against the SLRs on the Function Definitions and in the Requirements Catalogue. Where SLRs cannot be met the Physical Data Design is optimised and the resource times recalculated. If the SLRs cannot be met readily then consideration should be given to changing them. This is an iterative process and it must be remembered that changes to the data design made to meet SLRs may cause storage constraints to be broken.

Chapter 4
The interface between SSADM and capacity planning

After Step 640 the Service Level Requirements are carried forward to be incorporated in the Service Level Agreement to be negotiated between the users and IT service providers after system implementation.

Step 670 — This Step reviews the Physical Design. Capacity planning can be used at this point to assist the review process by checking whether service levels and design constraints can be met.

4.3.3 Calculation of data storage requirements

The Physical Data Design is produced in Step 640. This provides a full specification of how the information requirements of the system are to be implemented in the target environment, as specified in the Technical Environment Description. It may take the form of a database schema. Capacity planning can be used to produce precise projections of data storage requirements.

4.3.4 Creation of workload models

If capacity modelling has been used in earlier stages, workload models will already have been created. The workload models can be reworked using the Physical Data Design and the Program Specifications (contained in the Function Component Implementation Map).

4.3.5 Information sources

Annex B lists the capacity planning information requirements cross-referenced with the relevant SSADM logical design products and the entries in those products from which the information can be derived.

Annex C lists the capacity planning information requirements cross-referenced with the relevant SSADM physical design products and the entries in those products from which the information can be derived.

Annexes

Annex A
SSADM Stage 4 (Technical System Options) information sources

A SSADM Stage 4 (Technical System Options) information sources

SSADM Product	information content	capacity planning use
Function Definitions	Function Description	To give an overview of processing To determine sequence of off-line processing To identify message output device
	Events and Enquiries	To identify tasks & to reference the detail of processing in the ELHs, ECDs, and EAPs
	Type of Function	To identify type of task (on-line/off-line)
	I/O Structures references	To identify I/OStructures for the function
	Volumetrics (including peaks and troughs)	To determine task arrival rates To determine (together with I/O Structures) message arrival rates
	Service Level Requirements	To evaluate the capacity planning results
I/O Structure	I/O Structure input and output elements	To identify message pairs To reference the I/O Structure elements on the I/O Structure Descriptions
I/O Structure Descriptions	I/O Structure Element Data Items Comment	To determine the probability of an effect occurring if it is optional or the average number of occurrences of an iterated effect To determine message size and arrival rate
Entity Life Histories (ELHs)	Operations	To identify for a task the type of access to an entity to help estimate the disk access overhead
	Volatility of entities (derived from the insert/delete/amend operations)	To estimate access volumes
Effect Correspondence Diagrams (ECDs)	Entities affected by an event	To identify entity types accessed by task
	*Number of effect occurrences	To determine the number of accesses to estimate duration of processor occupancy
Enquiry Access Paths (EAPs)	Entities accessed by an enquiry	To identify entity types accessed by task
Required System LDM	Number of occurrences of each entity Relationship volumes	To determine the number of entity accesses per task To identify navigation paths for tasks (ECDs)
Entity Descriptions	List of Entities Number of occurrences of each entity Data Items in each Entity	To assist in the calculation of data storage requirements To reference Data Items in the Data Catalogue to carry out sizing
Requirements Catalogue	Cross-system service levels Priority	To evaluate the capacity planning results To identify the tasks to be modelled
Data Catalogue	Length of data items	To assist in the calculation of data storage requirements To determine the size of messages
User Role/Function Matrix	The dialogues required by a user role Critical functions	To identify the dialogues to be built and together with the I/O Structures and Function Definitions to determine their complexity To identify the tasks to be modelled

* see section 4.1, Creation of workload models, to determine how this information can be derived.

SSADM and Capacity Planning

B SSADM Stage 5 (Logical Design) information sources

SSADM Product	information content	capacity planning use
Function Definitions	Function Description References to events and enquiries Function type Service level requirements Volumetrics	To determine off-line processing sequence To identify tasks To identify on-line and off-line tasks To evaluate capacity planning results To determine task arrival rates from process model and enquiry model arrival rates
Physical Data Design	Type of file/DB used Physical files (entities) Block/page type Block/page size Organisation of entities into physical groups Record types and size Index & relationship overheads Volumetrics Direct access mechanisms Mechanisms used to implement primary and secondary relationships	To identify the DBMS/File handler used To determine navigation paths To determine File/DB size & arrangement " " " To size the database and estimate the number of disk accesses per physical read To estimate the number of records accessed To estimate the number of physical reads for each logical read
Technical Environment Description	Description of the physical environment (including hardware and software)	To determine the hardware configuration To estimate software overheads
Update Process Models	Operations List	To identify the entities/records accessed To determine the type of access To determine the number of disk accesses (derived from the operations and the volumes on the Physical Data Design)
Enquiry Process Model	Operations List	To identify the entities/records accessed To determine the type of access To determine the number of disk accesses (derived from the operations and the volumes on the Physical Data Design)
Requirements Catalogue	Service Level Requirements	To evaluate the capacity planning results

Annex C
SSADM Stage 6 (Physical Design) information sources

C SSADM Stage 6 (Physical Design) information sources

SSADM Product	information content	capacity planning use
Function Definitions	Function Description References to events and enquiries Function type Service Level Requirements Volumetrics	To determine batch processing sequence To identify tasks To identify on-line and off-line tasks To evaluate capacity planning results To determine process and enquiry arrival rates which are used to determine task arrival rates
Physical Data Design	Type of file/DB used Physical files (entities) Block/page type Block/page size Organisation of entities into physical groups Record types and size Index & relationship overheads Volumetrics Direct access points Mechanisms used to implement primary and secondary relationships	To identify the DBMS/File handler used To determine navigation paths To determine File/DB size & arrangement " " " To size the database and estimate the number of disk accesses per physical read To estimate the number of records accessed To estimate the number of physical reads for each logical read "
Technical Environment Description	Description of the physical environment (including hardware and software) Screen handler	To determine the hardware configuration To estimate software overheads To determine the processing required for dialogue and menu displays
Function Component Implementation Map (FCIM)	Programs/Module specifications Function components (eg UPMs and EPMs) Common processing Error handling Physical dialogues Physical screen layouts Type and no of records accessed Type of access Data items accessed Sorting requirements	To identify how functions and thus UPMs & EPMs are organised into programs & off-line sequencing of tasks To identify tasks and type of processing carried out " " " I/O processing, message size To calculate disk access time and CPU time from the number and type of accesses " "
Process Data Interface	Update and enquiry views	To determine the physical accesses needed to execute a logical access
Requirements Catalogue	Service Level Requirements	To evaluate capacity planning results

Bibliography

Information Systems Guides The Information Systems Guides, published by CCTA, are available from John Wiley & Sons Ltd, Baffins Lane, Chichester PO19 1UD.

The following guides provide more details on topics referenced in this publication:

    B2   The Feasibility Study
           ISBN 0 471 92527 6

    B3   The Full Study
           ISBN 0 471 92528 4

    B8   Systems Engineering
           ISBN 0 471 92533 0

    C1   Services Management
           ISBN 0 471 92534 9

    C6   Capacity Planning
           ISBN 0 471 92539 X

IT Infrastructure Library The IT Infrastructure Library is published by HMSO and is available from HMSO Books (P9D), St Crispins, Duke Street, Norwich NR3 1PD.

The following modules are referenced in this publication:

Availability Management
ISBN 0 113 30551 6

Service Level Management
ISBN 0 113 30521 4

Capacity Management
ISBN 0 113 30544 3

SSADM documentation The SSADM Version 4 Reference Manual is published by NCC and is available from The Publications Manager, National Computer Centre Ltd, Oxford Road, Manchester M1 7ED. ISBN 1 85554 004 5.

Glossary

Analysis of Requirements
This forms the Module Product from the Requirements Analysis Module. It consists of the Current Services Description, Requirements Catalogue, User Catalogue and the Selected Business Option.

business needs
Those fundamental activities, processes and information that must be provided in order to meet the statutory obligations and business objectives of the department.

Business System Option (BSO) – technique
The means by which users agree the new application's desired functionality with developers. BSOs are used to define the functionality needs and the boundary for the system, with reference to the business needs.

Business Systems Specification
In Systems Engineering terms the Business Systems Specification is the product of the requirements definition and logical design process.

Capacity Management
A set of techniques, supported by software tools, designed to facilitate the smooth, progressive, rational and economic provision, and the efficient use, of IT capacity to maintain an acceptable level of service in the face of changing workloads arising from the demands of an organisation's business plan.

Data Flow Diagram (DFD)
A diagrammatic representation of the bodies of information which an information system will handle, showing the logical inter-relationships between them.

effect
The change caused to a single entity because of a single event. An effect can be one of four kinds: create (birth), modify (update), logical delete (death) or update of state indicators.

Effect Correspondence Diagram (ECD)
Shows all the effects an event has on data within the system and how those effects impact on each other.

Effect Correspondence Diagrams provide the access path details for update functions which is used in logical design activities.

Enquiry Access Path (EAP)	The route through the Logical Data Model from an entry point to the entity, or entities, required for a particular enquiry function.
Enquiry Process Model (EPM)	Consists of a structure diagram for an enquiry processing requirement and the associated Operations List. The structure is based on the Enquiry Access Path.
entity	Something, whether concrete or abstract, which is of importance to the area of business being investigated.
Entity Life History (ELH)	Structure diagrams for all entity life histories identified within the system. An Entity Life History is a structure combining all possible 'lives' of every possible occurrence of the entity.
event	An event is identified as whatever triggers a process (on a Data Flow Diagram) to update the values or status of the system. An event may cause more than one entity to be changed.
Feasibility Options	The set of Feasibility Options which is compiled so that a selection can be made. Each option documents the functions to be incorporated and details implementation requirements. Each description is textual with some planning information.
Feasibility Report	1 The final report resulting from a Feasibility Study; it forms the basis of management decisions about the future of the system under study. 2 This documents the possible approaches to a system development and assesses the impact of each so that the most appropriate way ahead can be fully investigated.
Feasibility Study	A short assessment of an information system proposed in the IS strategy.
Function Component Implementation Map	A classification and specification of all implementation fragments for all function components defined in the Function Definitions to meet the processing requirements.
Function Definitions	The packaging of all details about functions to be included in the Requirements Specification. These details are further expanded during physical design activities.

Glossary

Impact Analysis	Describes the effects of the option (business or technical) on the user environment and will cover issues concerned with organisation, procedures and implementation factors. This product is used to document the ramifications of following a particular course of action.
information management	The means by which an organisation maximises the efficiency with which it plans, collects, organises, uses, controls, disseminates and disposes of its information, and by which it ensures that the value and potential value of that information is identified and exploited to the fullest extent.
information system	Any procedure or process, with or without IT support, which provides a way of acquiring, storing, processing, or disseminating information. Information systems include applications and their supporting infrastructure components.
information system lifecycle	A collective term for the various stages that an information system goes through during its existence, from its initial conception through to its final decommissioning.
infrastructure	Refers to both IT infrastructure (the hardware, software, and computer-related communications that support the ongoing provision of the IT service) and/or organisational infrastructure (management, organisation, finance). Infrastructure systems are a sub-set of information systems.
IT provider	The source, either internal or external to the organisation, which provides the IT services required to perform the business of the organisation.
Logical Data Model (LDM)	Provides an accurate model of the information requirements of all or part of an organisation. This serves as a basis for file and database design, but is independent of any specific implementation technique or product.
	The Logical Data Model consists of a Logical Data Structure, Entity Descriptions and Relationship Descriptions. Associated descriptions of attribute/data items and grouped domains are maintained in the Data Catalogue.

Physical Data Design	The definition for the physical database which is to be implemented. The design is developed in two steps; the first produces a 'first-cut' design based on applying rules about the DBMS to the Required System Logical Data Model; the second is a design optimised for performance reasons.
Physical Design	It is the Module Product from the Physical Design Module which defines the data and processing elements of the implementable system.
Physical Design Strategy	Documents all aspects relating to designing the physical implementation of the application. This includes all planning documentation.
Project	A project is regarded as having the following characteristics: • a defined and unique set of technical products to meet the business needs • a corresponding set of activities to construct those products • a certain amount of resources • a finite lifespan • an organisational structure with defined responsibilities.
Required System Logical Data Model	Provides the detail of the proposed system information requirements. It is developed during the Requirements Specification and Logical System Specification Modules. See also *Logical Data Model*.
Requirement	Describes a required feature of the proposed system. Requirements may be functional (describing what the system should do) or non-functional (describing how a facility should be provided, or how well, or to what level of quality).
Requirements Specification	The Module Product from the Requirements Specification Module, packaging all of the details which are required in order to decide upon the technical direction of the project.

Glossary

service	A set of related functions provided by an IT system; it is perceived and operated by users as a coherent and self-contained entity. A service may range from access to a single application program to the use of one or more global facilities: for example, a transaction processing system, a suite of batch programs, or a print system.
Service Level Agreement (SLA)	A written agreement or 'contract' between users and the IT Services Manager, which documents the agreed service levels for an IT service.
Service Level Requirement (SLR)	A statement of requirements as to the quality (including reliability and availability) of a service. Later this is formalised as a Service Level Agreement.
System Description	Shows how the Requirements Specification is met by the Technical Environment Description for a particular Technical System Option. In many cases the major decisions in this area will have already been taken in choosing a Business System Option.
task	In the context of capacity planning, those portions of processing that are important enough to be modelled; based in early SSADM Stages on Events, and later on process outlines.
Technical System Option (TSO) – technique	The means by which users agree the new application's implementation strategy incorporating the desired functionality, as defined in the Requirements Specification. Several Technical System Options are developed and one is selected (or combined elements from several). This gives the technical direction for future development.
Technical System Options	The set of Technical System Options which has been developed so that the system development direction can be chosen. Each option documents the functions to be incorporated and details implementation requirements. Each description is textual with some planning information. Functional elements are taken directly from the Requirements Specification.
transaction	A single exchange of information between the user and the computer; for example, enquiring about a particular customer's details, or inputting details of a new customer order.

transaction processing	A mode of computer service, where many non-technical users have simultaneous access to corporate processes and files. Airline booking is a typical transaction processing service. Clerks are able to enquire on the availability of seats, and to make bookings on demand. They do not need any technical knowledge of the service, since they send and receive information via special forms on the screen. Files are updated in real time, so that information is always current.
Update Process Model (UPM)	Is a structure diagram for the update (event) processing and the associated operations list. This is based on the Entity Life Histories, which provide a data-orientated view of the system, and the associated Effect Correspondence Diagrams, which provide an event-orientated or process-orientated view of the system.
user	Any person who actually uses a system.
workload	In the context of capacity modelling, a series of forecasts which detail the estimated resource usage over the agreed planning horizon(s). *Workload* would generally be broken down to represent discrete business applications and further subdivided into types of work (interactive, timesharing, batch).

Printed in the United Kingdom for HMSO
Dd295384 5/92 C8 G3390 10170